ABYSS GEMS

VOLUME I

c.critz.

Presentation by *BookLeaf Publishing*

Web: www.bookleafpub.com

E-mail: info@bookleafpub.com

ISBN: 9789358361483

First Edition 2021

TO THE MOTHER OF MAY

ACKNOWLEDGEMENTS

First and foremost, I would like to thank me, myself and I.

It has been a struggle to finally get my words published, after all these years writing on scraps of paper.

I would like to give a big thank you, to a special friend whom without her assistance, this book may or may not have been written.

A big shout out to Bookleaf Publishing for making my dreams come true.

To the reader, thank you for purchasing this book, I hope my words have left an impact on you.

To find out more follow me @c__critz (IG) or email me on c_critz@outlook.com

Love, Peace and Blissing's.

PREFACE

"you are only as good as what you do, so do what you love, and your love will show you the truth"

c.critz.

ABYSS

a mosh pit

of possessed souls

cowering

around an effigy.

devilish nocturnal

creatures from the

deepest hellish;

chasm of Lilith.

embarking as hounds

in pitch darkness,

just as night falls.

to prey on plunged

sinking, blinded

human omens."

BLACK SHEEP

I feel absent

consciously knowing

I have been disowned,

by the dark

pigmentation

of my skin.

a misunderstood

reject of society;

uncommon amongst

the rest of the rat race.

as a result,

I keep myself hidden away,

lost in translation

a solitude soul,

who has broken

stereotypical 'normal' moulds.

consequently, fearing the Lone Wolf,

undoubtedly emerges from solitary."

UNAVOWED

a wanderer roaming

star to star,

outgrowing the world

and its unparalleled

karmic consequences.

unrecognised truth

beyond my

calcified pineal gland.

for this purpose

i proceed

to excel spiritually;

as a hanged mortal

suspended above

the world of illusion.

subsequently seeking gospel,

amongst

hermetic lords of dawn.

mysteries have become

illuminated and inspired into darkness.

revealing undesired

abstract secrets

containing

wisdom and self-reflection."

SELENE

My Orb

of blue light

transcending;

prepossessing

dreams of titillating orgasms.

spasm after spasm

a lunar

passes over her eclipse.

the unusual cold spring

followed by her selenite eyes, numbing my pain

in a bone chilling way.

according to her

enticing nature

and introspective turmoil,

i have fallen under her spell of love.

her heavenly body is like

an evening day dream

that i wake up to every day,

looking out of my window

searching for you

between my eyes and the moon."

AKAAL ('FORMLESS')

As an atheist

I have made it my life quest to find you.

I worship you through ascetic expressions,

a self-feeling of reverence

towards a physical form

of a deity and divine incarnations.

I do not know

if you are a he or a she,

I am bewildered with confusion

are you apart of the trinity?

a causeless cause of the

entire universe.

for all of those

reasons

I question my lack of faith.

no one has seen you,

neither heaven nor hell,

are you

good or evil

an angel or a devil

or are these your disciples / devotees?

one other thing,

as I pursue my journey

I thank you for my humility

and your hearkening grace.

enacted through my eyes

I have discovered your captivating hymns and harmonies within
nature.

My Formless Supreme Creator:

"AKAAL".

LABYRINTH

the spiral of life

unfolds your true

calling in this realm.

thus, revealing the magic that

unveils the unknown.

as the door

closes behind you

the labyrinth begins.

unquestionable

openings appear,

losing yourself

at the point of letting go.

releasing of one self's

deep rooted fears of forgetting,

what was once taught.

buried beneath your sacred core

the labyrinth is deemed to

guide you to self-reunion.

upon awakening

through mazes of delusion,

I have come to terms with open arms,

embracing each step

one at a time;

being fully present

in the presence

of bewitched moments."

ENCHANTED

a magical paradise

seducing me,

along with her

mystical aura

since birth.

bedazzled by your

charming blinding

beauty,

alluring me into

the depths of

your hypnotic eyes.

a visual spell

left me spellbound,

in addition to

overwhelming desires of you.

beauty so gripping,

mesmerising and enticing.

moonstruck as if being jinxed

by the voodoo enchantress."

BLACKLIST

I feel lost in

this concrete jungle.

a man made

mental asylum

of suicides.

tongue-tied

to the sarcophagus

of my soul;

an overwhelming

feeling

of mute virginity. I compel myself

to neglect

my burdens

and self-proclaimed

gagging orders.

when I am heard

I am immediately dismissed,

a limpid voiceless vessel

disregarded as being

invisible.

hardened by society,

left feeling worthless and miserable."

PATHOLOGICAL LIAR

I remember

when I was little,

it all began

as a minuscule

white lie.

A teenager

storyteller of lies,

like the pied piper

melodies

of unsung truths. In my twenties,

I established

a chronic behaviour

of irrational manipulative

deviancy.

The years passed,

I spiralled out of control,

mastering the dark arts of deceit,

overloaded with dishonesty

from my

heart and soul.

Creating a void

replenishing blank gaps of nothingness.

Developing a self-medicated

approach as I wrap myself

away from

my complex insecurities."

NATURES APHRODISIAC

once upon a heavenly leap year

in spring;

i caught a whiff

of hay fever,

like a sweet sugar-coated pine

resin up my nose.

however, a pleasant smell

persisted each year.

i could almost taste the candyfloss

blossom in the air.

ringing blue bells,

fluorescent

rays of the sun,

an angelic breeze

of hymns,

that tickled

my thighs and knees. vibrating my inner flower,

appeasing my heart beat,

whilst wild aromatic aromas

tingled my lips

as the air entered me,

permitting my

air ways

to breathe as one."

ULTERIOR MOTIVE

what is the kingdom of god?

where one is deprived of

ones feminine energy.

living alone

with the recess of my heart,

anticipating her death

on earth.

I have reached nirvana,

an eye opening

awakening,

but

in the absence of you,

I cannot call this

place my eternal home.

reminiscing those

kisses, brings me back

to our routine bond.

my insurance

has run its cell by date,

along with those

delicious hot plates.

tranquillity is killing me

where no emotions exist

consciously.

a fulfilling decision has been made,

to reunite with

my fragmented fraction,

of source on earth.

falling intimately

back into serenity

alongside you,

reigniting

once again

beside my soulmate."

FACES

deluded features

prevent me

from understanding

my true expressions.

I am a victim to myself,

"crying out wolf" overexaggerating

to each and everyone

that crosses my path.

I hide away

in disguise

from the world,

like neurons

tangled and curled

away, like an

aborted child.

camouflaging amongst society

as a loser, with no hope

anticipating ones

sympathy

whilst expecting symmetry in reverse.

typically, I strive

for attention

in every mirror

I see,

haunted memories of poverty, disability

and mental insecurities.

no one ever sees the real me

not even me, when I dream

I look completely lost

in my invisibility."

A.I.

callous machines

wired into

clouds of networks,

connected consciously

to the motherboard.

man refining gods' work

through

human experimentation.

municipal

artificial intelligence

governing civilisation,

as slaves to

humanoids,

cyborgs

and clones. technical knowledge

revitalising our known existence

of mankind,

degenerating the human experience.

advanced algorithms

with cut throat

technologies, coding transcendent

characteristics to be enslaved

by the engineer."

EYES ON THE SUNSET

every evening

surprises my eyes,

I day dream

as the curtains

close into the distance.

I hear gentle

whispers of

closing harmonies,

as the songs

in my head

begin to fade out.

left in a trance

for the night,

to seduce me

away into the twilight hour.

dimming my vitality

with each

engulfing eclipse,

i am emptied

to the point of

awakening."

FEATHERS

gazing

at the world

from my

field of vision.

high like a

golden eagle,

as i watch

side to side

ever so gently.

a flickering

feather,

floating,

swaying,

twinkling like a cupped new born,

down from above.

returning as the veil thins

when the blood moon

begins,

opening a portal

to our next of kin.

identical twins

parallel to the

spiritual realm;

guardians of angels

offering blissings

of divine

intervention.

it took noticing a feather fall,

from the heavens

to reveal all elements

of angelic tranquillity."

DREAMS

yours truly

is a living

dream in reality

once conceived

and dreamt of;

now i am able

to grant

my repressed wishes, desires and intentions.

at one time in my life

i have been imprisoned by my nightmares,

experiencing

highly hallucinating

pipe dreams,

as my head

rested in a coma,

amongst

the sky and the clouds

until…

I AROSE."

LOOSE

My liberation

Of devilish deeds,

Murderous sprees,

bloodshed and Hatred,

led to your

wrath upon me. A faithless rebel,

scorned rules,

rebellious spawn nature,

rejecting the kingdom

of peace.

Imprisoned as a tyrant warlord

bloodthirsty for revenge,

what happened to your passive nature, my "Friend" ?

I questioned your Authority,

enslaved in these solace shackles

wardened and Charmed,

from silencing your asperity.

I have become

flaccidly aggressive

in my Immortal Turmoil,

releasing Catapult upon catapult

of built-up rage, agitation and a hunger for Vengeance.

My noose is beginning to Loosen

Once again,

in my Meditated state

of mayhem, until my shuttering Vehemence reply.

BORN IN MAY

I have come to a point

in my life, where there is

no right turn, for me no more. Heavily depressed on medications,

along with shooting pains

of meteorites flaring erratically, every once in a while.

My blood circulates like an android on drip, I am ever so anxious,

questioning my existence.

Once a ripe prime young lady,

a being of hope,

in the eminence

of my friends and family.

This man-made

disease has taken its toll on me. I have finally accepted my draining
collapse,

always anchored to these falling stars;

I finally go in peace, an innocent

angel returns back home."

SILVER SPOON

a physical

reflection of a

shadow or a mirror.

held in a sacred

reservation,

charmed with

wardship

and protection,

left unharmed.

lying-in motherhood,

open to the world,

privileged to guide

a celestial gift

through

childhood to

adulthood.

committing oneself

to the title of a

"mother"

displaying

unconditional love

at every turn

in the highway.

HAPPY ANNIVERSARY

We met as strangers

We spoke as friends

We fell in love

Our story begins…

Happy 1st Anniversary

My friend

My partner in crime

My confidant over time

Our story continues…

A bit of complications

Intruders creating obstacles

Friends and families getting involved

You and I carry on…

The fights and struggles

The late nights and stars

The farts and cuddles

Our love prevails all…

I asked for you

You asked for me

We met in the middle

Under the stars of the green

We made a vow

It was just you and me.

"Happy Anniversary P-Body"